Toby the Farm Dog

Remembering a Friend

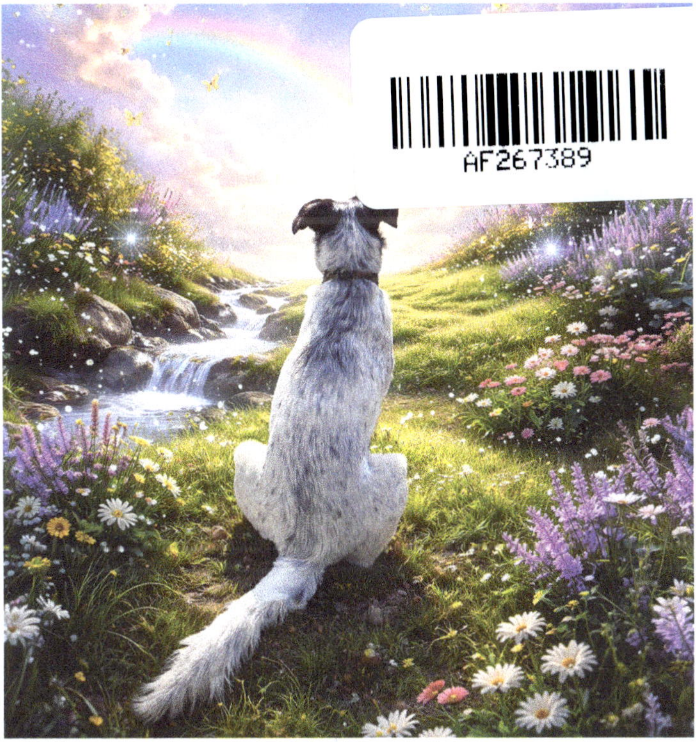

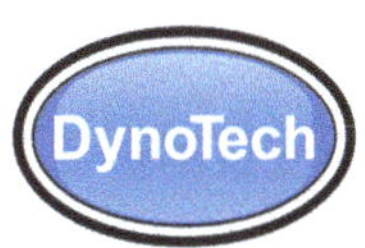

Author: Donna Lindahl

Editor: Dave Carlson

DynoTech

DynoTech Publishing, Colorado Springs, CO

Edited and published by Dave Carlson, DynoTech Publishing, Colorado Springs, Colorado, United States of America. (www.dynotech.com)

ISBN: 978-1-885708-22-9 (Paperback)
ISBN: 978-1-885708-36-6 (eBook/EPUB)

Library of Congress Control Number: 2026909924

First Printing: April 2026

Remembering Toby

Final Picture of Toby the Farm Dog

Sadly, our beloved Toby the Farm Dog crossed the rainbow bridge on April 8, 2026. An old head injury finally took its toll.

Toby the Farm Dog

Hi. My name is Toby.
I hope you enjoy reading about my world.

I live on a farm in Missouri, USA. That's why humans call me "Toby the Farm Dog."
If you were a dog who could read, you'd be laughing on the floor right now. That was a good dog joke!

I help with loading the bales. OK, you're right. I just supervise. And, I agree with you; my human friend is doing an amazing job.

When horses eat hay I keep them safe.

I watch over them from a distance.

I also check on them and keep them safe when
they nap in the hay.

Of course, I'm always prepared for when they wake up and are ready to get up and play. I like to play with all my farm friends.

Sometimes I take a nap too, especially when the sun is warm (but not too hot). When it's too hot, I find a farm friend who has enough sense to nap in the shade.

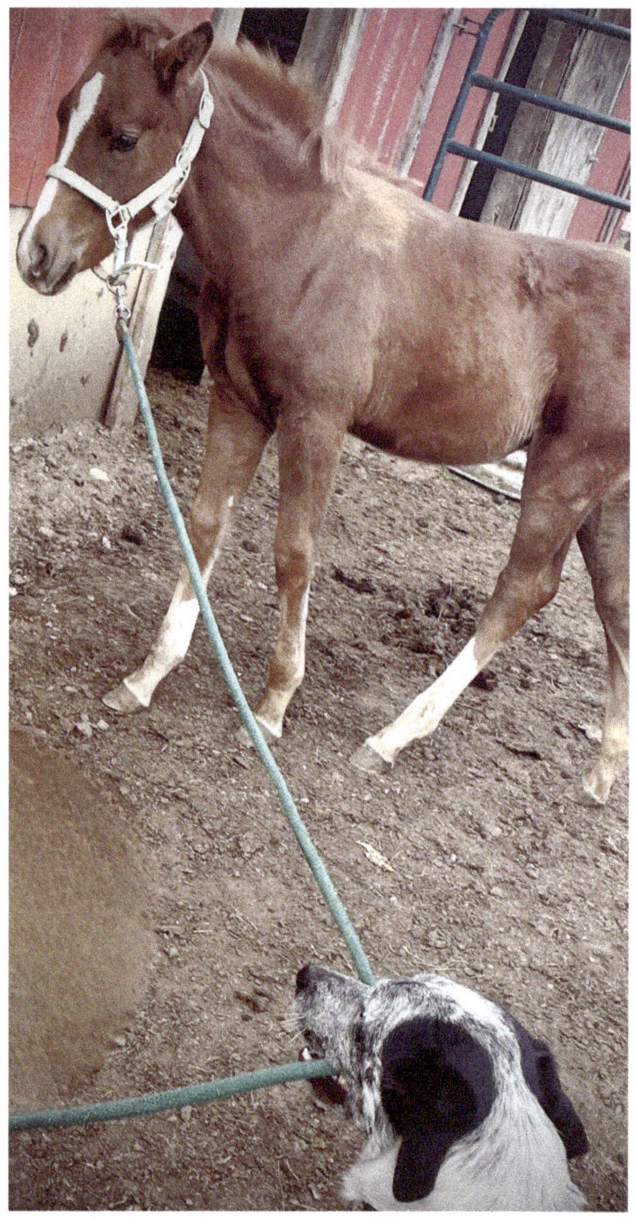

I can lead horses with a rope, but sometimes they act like my donkey friend and get stubborn. I pull hard, but they don't move.

I keep mama horse and her baby safe. I like baby horses and think they're very cute. Do you think so too?

I like helping people. I'm stretching so I don't hurt myself when I pick up the chainsaw. My human friend is trying to be serious and not laugh, because he knows the chainsaw is too heavy for me to lift. He knows I'm bluffing and just trying to look tough.

I can carry branches, especially the ones that are lighter than a chainsaw.

I can carry pieces of wood almost as big as I am. This one is big enough to add to the fireplace woodpile.

I help move firewood in the moving box called "GATOR." Sometimes the firewood is what I carried across the yard. No, I still can't read, but I remembered my human friend called the moving box GATOR. That must be its name, like my name is Toby.

Sometimes I try to drive. Don't laugh, I could learn. Inside the human house, I was watching a box with a window that let me see dogs doing some amazing things. One of them grabbed a ball in his mouth. He jumped up and dropped the ball in a basket high over his head, I thought, "I could do that."

My human boss says I have to ride, NOT drive. He does ALL the driving. He won't let me drive even when I stare at him with my "tough dog" face. He just stares back at me and doesn't even blink.

Sometimes after we move firewood, cold white stuff called "snow" falls from the sky and covers the ground. My People Parents got nice snow boots for me to keep my paws warm in the snow.

I'm glad I have snow boots just my size. Now, if I can only figure out how to walk while wearing these things, all would be great.

I give advice about farm machines. You can see how happy my human friend is about my advice. I think he likes it when I help him like this. It makes me feel good, too.

"Go for a ride in the truck?"
BEST WORDS EVER!

But, People Mom won't let me drive either. I sit in the back seat, where I can keep an eye on her to make sure she does it right. I don't think I'd like it if the truck made a BIG BUMP by hitting something.

Are we there yet? ... Are we there yet?
Oh ... we haven't left yet.
Can we go now? ... Can we go now?
A truck ride is my FAVORITE activity!

At least, if we aren't going yet, I have a nice, comfy place to wait and relax.
    {*In a whisper ...*} Can we go now?

I'm a good helper. I carry tools. I even get the handle wet and slippery, so my human friend doesn't get blisters. (*I know that word too, because I heard my human friend say he doesn't like them.*)

Toby Flashback

I remember the first day on the farm. I had never been away from home before, and I was afraid. My new human gave me a small teddy bear and it helped me start feeling a little bit safe at my new home.

Toby Flashback

I was so traumatized, I was afraid to move. The nice human who gave me my first cuddly buddy, laid down on the ground with me and rubbed my ears. I felt safer.

Toby Flashback

The next stop at my new home was to the deck attached to the big human house. When my new human friend put me on the deck, there was a HUGE teddy bear and doggy toys waiting for me there. I was surprised, but happy.

Toby Flashback

I was soooo tired, but I was afraid to sleep. Now, on the deck at my new home, I felt safe. I was able to take my first nap on the deck, comforted by my new blanket and cuddly deck buddies.

I help people fix things. Ok ... so I just watch, but that's good morale support. What's this on the hat? It smells good, so I need to lick it off to make everything go back to the way it's supposed to smell. What?! That's what dog's do! I can't violate a primary canine rule:

"If it smells good or yucky, lick it."

When I'm not busy helping my human friends, I run and play with my ball. I love playing with my ball.

My human friend helps me play with my ball. Sometimes after playing with the ball, I get a ride in the farm truck. In case you haven't figured it out yet, ... I LOVE riding in a farm truck. It's my favorite thing. (But, not my ONLY favorite thing; I like to eat too!)

My favorite outside toy is my ball. My favorite inside toy is "Monkey-Horse." Yup! There are two of them with the same name.
BEST TOY EVER!

I like to share my toys and doggy bed ONLY with special humans, like my little human friend Dalton.

I love to sleep with my Monkey-Horse "twins" in my inside doggy bed. When I wake up they're right where I left them. Well, at least close to where I left them. People Mom tells me sometimes I move a lot when I sleep.

I want to let you in on a little "doggy secret." This is my special "can we play" face. It almost always works on humans after I train them.

Sometimes I use a different "can we play" face. My humans are smart, and, eventually, they learn to recognize different faces.

I've learned manners. This is my specail "please" expression I use when I REALLY want to impress a human.

Of course, I have another special "please" expression, as well. I sneak in a little bit of "anticipated appreciation." Some humans act like it's an extra-special expression, so I save this expression for very special occasions and extra-special humans, like Grandma D. (*She's one of my favorite human friends who lives in Colorado.*)

I like to play with Duck. He's my favorite animal play friend, but he's not as cute as a baby horse or a baby puppy. I think I like baby puppies more that baby horses, but maybe that's just 'cause I'm a dog.

Duck likes to play with me, but, sometimes he plays kind of rough. I don't like when he hits me with his beak or flaps his wings in my face. I thought about biting him one time, but I'd never do that to my best animal friend.

Sometimes Duck flaps his wings and flies off the ground. That always scares me a little bit. I can't get used to it when he takes off into the sky and leaves me on the ground.

Playing makes us thirsty, so we put water in a tank. Actually, Duck just watches and I put the hose in the tank (that's not my ONLY trick). But, I need help from one of my human friends to turn on the water, becasue I don't have what they call "opposable thumbs."

Duck and I take a drink. Ah ... that fresh cool water sure tastes good after a hard play session with Duck. What? No, that stuff in the water doesn't bother me. Remember, I'm a dog.

Sometimes a drink isn't enough, so I join Duck in the tub to cool off.

Duck likes to take a splashy bath.

Duck was having so much fun with his splashy bath, I decided to try it when he was done. How 'bout that? I like to take a splashy bath too.

Sometimes I like to play with a ball in the water. But, I don't think the ball likes to play with me. It just keeps rolling over and over in the water and won't come closer to the edge of the tub. If I play too hard, it just runs away to the other side of the tub where I can't reach it.

Duck shares his supper with me. I'm a dog, so I'll eat almost anything. However, I like my dog food better (especially doggy cookies). At least it was nice that my friend shared with me.

After supper we take a rest to let our yummy food settle. Resting is almost always a good thing.

Sometimes Duck and I like to rest, and watch the farm activities.

I don't always rest with Duck, because I have a nice doggy bed on the porch. It's a great way to relax and enjoy the view.

I can even relax and STILL keep an eye on what's happening in the yard.

Ocassionally, it's a good idea to stop and smell the flowers.

After taking time to smell the flowers, it's also a good time to lie down and get ready for a nap in the flowers.

I go to the house when it gets dark. It makes me feel safe and happy when my human friend hugs and pets me.

I like reading books before bedtime. I like to get really close, so I can see the pictures.

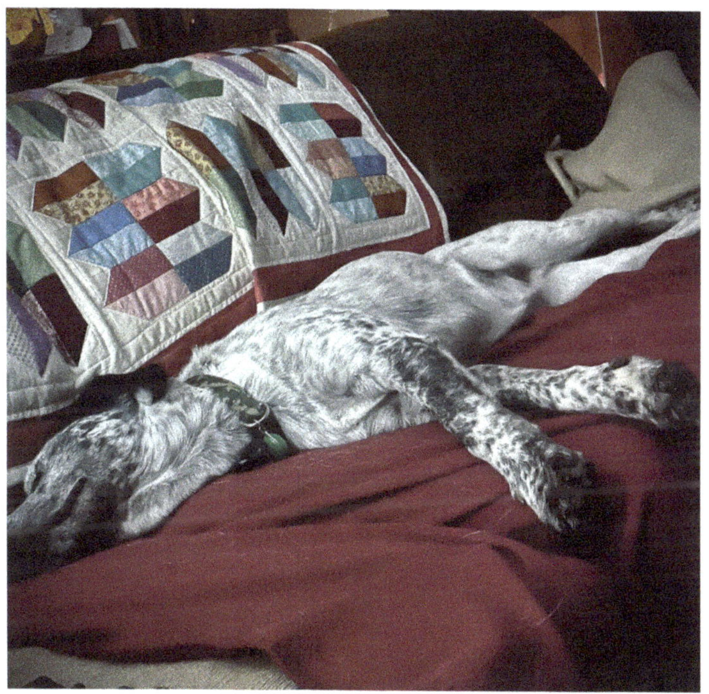

I'm tired from my busy day. It's nice to have a big, comfy couch where I can stretch out. Of course, I let my human friends use it when I don't need it to stretch out.

So, I say "Good Night" and fall asleep.

It's time for a happy doggy dream about green grass, pretty flowers (that don't make me sneeze), clean water in a brook, just enough clouds to make shady places on the ground (yet let plenty of sunshine in), and a beautiful, colorful rainbow bridge for me to jump over, when it's time.

💔

Author Biography
Donna Lindahl

www.donnalindahl.com

Donna Lindahl grew up in a small mining town in northern Minnesota where her dad was a photographer and her mom was a photojournalist. From an early age Donna watched her parents describe people's lives with pictures and words.

"Get the story" became Donna's focus from a young age as she helped her dad process photographs in the darkroom and spent time with her mom talking about stories and news assignments.

During college, Donna worked as a newspaper photographer. As an Army wife, she worked as a dog groomer. She describes her "best day ever" as when she got a job at a military riding stable as a trail guide and "entered the world of horse."

Donna is now retired on her horse farm where photo-ops and stories abound. Each person and animal has something to share, and Donna wants to "get the story."

Toby and Donna

www.donnalindahl.com/toby/

www.ingramcontent.com/pod-product-compliance
Lightning Source LLC
Chambersburg PA
CBHW050044040726
47599CB00015B/1788